T0368576

LIFE
PAINKILLERS

AMR MUNEER DAHAB

AuthorHouse™
1663 Liberty Drive
Bloomington, IN 47403
www.authorhouse.com
Phone: 833-262-8899

Because of the dynamic nature of the Internet, any web addresses or links contained in this book may have changed
since publication and may no longer be valid. The views expressed in this work are solely those of the author and do not
necessarily reflect the views of the publisher, and the publisher hereby disclaims any responsibility for them.

Any people depicted in stock imagery provided by Getty Images are models,
and such images are being used for illustrative purposes only.
Certain stock imagery © Getty Images.

This book is printed on acid-free paper.

ISBN: 978-1-6655-2458-2 (sc)
ISBN: 978-1-6655-2459-9 (e)

Print information available on the last page.

Published by AuthorHouse 04/29/2021

authorHOUSE®

To those who seek comfort and tranquility in life, without exaggerating the promise of a perfect treatment.

CONTENTS

Preface vii

Boredom 1

Embarrassment..3

Obsession 5

Failure 7

Bad Luck 9

Satisfying Everyone 11

Betrayal 13

Failure to Pass a Job Interview 15

Loss of Your Job 17

Retirement 19

A Romantic Relationship Ends...21

The Demise of a Close Person...23

Injustice 25

An Intrigue 27

Ahead of Your Time..29

Cascade of Problems...31

Defeat 33

Abandon Principles 35

Routine 37

Self-Esteem Exaggeration 39

Aging 41

Whirlpool 43

PREFACE

Our basic issue dealing with life's difficulties begins when we expect these difficulties to be temporary. It is exacerbated when we imagine that each of them will be solved one day, once and for all.

This does not mean that we should surrender to the feeling that problems are our inevitable destiny in life. Rather, we must face problems as uninterrupted challenges and understand that the problem itself is being solved to reappear in one way or another. Thus, we must constantly be prepared to deal with the problem as it appears in any form at any time.

Life Painkillers introduces the problem and suggests the appropriate painkiller and treatment. Nevertheless, the book itself takes its title from the idea that what we consider a cure for the problem is in the long run nothing but a long-acting painkiller. Therefore, it is more appropriate to view all matters of life as temporary and repetitive at the same time. It is wise to move beyond the idea of the eternal solution and final treatment in favor of the principle of not despairing of continuous attempts to reach the best possible solutions to recurring and newly created problems alike.

BOREDOM

- **Symptom:** Feeling that today is like yesterday and the day before, and like tomorrow and the day after.

- **Diagnosis**: Chronic boredom.

- **Painkiller**:

  - It is important to believe that the happiness curve is fluctuating and cannot be stabilized at any level of satisfaction or discontent.

  - Have a look at any of your pending items lists for some old tasks. You might find something interesting to help you out of your boredom circle.

  - Avoid fabricating problems in response to your boredom, as this will be very regrettable when the boredom strike elapses.

  - It is a good idea to try doing some work that you normally become passive or even overbearing about.

- **Treatment**:

  - It doesn't make sense to be surprised when you have a fit of boredom. If you can't do something positive directly, just try to avoid giving in to the feeling of frustration.

- When boredom strikes you, even your favorite entertainment won't come to your rescue. Do not overuse any of your regular entertainment means. Give yourself some time to regain your balance and determine what exactly might help you to get out of the cycle of boredom calmly and safely this time.

- You cannot be busy all the time. But remember that the odds of boredom increase as the leisure time in your life increases.

- Be creative. Preset programs are of no use when you feel bored. You need to discover each boredom strike's own treatment.

- As the definition of happiness itself cannot be precisely determined, focus on contentment, adaptation, and coping, whatever the circumstances around you.

- It is good to get involved in some old activities and relationships that you have been cut off from for a long time. Make sure you will be able to fulfill the requirements of these activities and relationships later, after the boredom has passed. Resuming any activity or relationship that you have been disconnected from for a long time might cause further problems if careful reevaluation is not considered regarding the relationship details and future consequences.

EMBARRASSMENT

⌀ **Symptom:** You wish the earth would swallow you up or that you were not created at all.

⌀ **Diagnosis**: Feeling deeply embarrassed during an absurd situation in which you unintentionally fell.

⌀ **Painkiller**:

   ⌀ Think a little about what it might bring back to you when feeling embarrassed: Nothing useful. Isn't that enough to immediately stop giving in to that negative feeling?

   ⌀ No one intends to fall into an embarrassing situation. Do not overburden yourself with sharp remorse. Just try to draw lessons learned to avoid repeating the situation as much as possible.

   ⌀ It's fine to be considerate of others, but feeling deeply embarrassed means that you care more about people's opinions and reactions than you should. Be sure to differentiate between respecting others and submitting to the control of their opinions about you. That will help you evaluate situations wisely and overcome embarrassment quickly and in a healthy way when it occurs.

   ⌀ Remember similar embarrassing situations faced by others around you. Remember other embarrassing situations that happened to you, even if they were different. It is all over, so it is wise to let the current embarrassing situation go as you will not benefit from its prolongation.

🔘 Treatment:

🔘 Embarrassment is a feeling that remains as long as you allow it. It's okay to be somewhat sensitive toward others and different situations, but don't overdo it. Do not allow embarrassment to dominate you for more than a moment. And do not allow it to linger in force for hours. Start searching sincerely for a positive, practical response to the situation or the person without exaggerating the justification or urgency for the sake of quickly restoring things to the way they were. Do not forget to put some confidence in the time factor if the situation is somewhat complicated.

🔘 There is no doubt that each situation differs in its response. In general, take a moment to absorb the fleeting shock, and think about the most appropriate response. But beware of lagging behind. The longer you delay the response more than necessary, the more complex the situation is likely to become.

🔘 Beware of those who enjoy keeping you feeling awkward and work to inflame that feeling within you. Whatever their position in the situation that happened to you, cut off the road for them by showing your indifference and self-confidence, no matter how severe the situation and its aftermath.

🔘 Never bow in shame or defeat. Even if you are wrong, that only requires you to admit to the mistake and confront it to correct it. Always make sure to keep your head high. That will help you a lot, especially in embarrassing situations. That will be the dose of confidence you very much need in those moments. At all times, keep what you need during critical times with you.

OBSESSION

🔘 **Symptom:** Feeling that you are in a vicious circle that is driving you crazy.

🔘 **Diagnosis**: Countless failed attempts to quit a manifestation of an obsessive behavior in your daily life.

🔘 **Painkiller**:

  🔘 Never be ashamed of your obsessive behavior. You are not responsible for its innate presence inside you unless you allow it to fester.

  🔘 Do not let anxiety aggravate the problem; remember that the worst-case scenario is that you cannot get rid of your obsession. As you dealt with it throughout your life in the past, you can continue your life in the future despite your obsession.

  🔘 It will ease the matter for you to realize that everyone has his or her own obsessions. The differences between people in this regard ultimately can be viewed as a matter of quantity related mainly to the degree or severity of the obsession.

  🔘 Whatever the nature of your obsession, it will not be without positive aspects, such as high accuracy, clear organization, and great hygiene. As you strive hard to get rid of the obsessive behavior, do not forget to take advantage of these positive aspects and allow them to give you some of the confidence and satisfaction you desperately need to overcome your obsession.

🔘 **Treatment**:

🔘 Getting to the point where your obsessive behavior clearly draws the attention of those around you is a very critical sign. Avoid reaching this stage altogether, and if you are on the edge of it, back off immediately without further thinking.

🔘 Do not hesitate to seek help from those close to you who are known for their patience and wisdom.

🔘 It is hard to find them, but if you get the chance to approach any of those who have succeeded in getting rid of an obsession permanently, their experience will undoubtedly be inspiring. However, any practical, positive, and successful personality can be an indirect source of inspiration and very useful to you.

🔘 When you have the opportunity to make the decision to quit the obsession, seize it immediately. Do not wait for a special occasion to implement the decision. That will become an obsession itself.

🔘 Do not hesitate to seek help from a psychiatrist or a psychologist. Do not despair of trying again and again.

FAILURE

- **Symptom:** Feeling that you will never be able to do it and deciding to give up trying any further.

- **Diagnosis**: An awful failure.

- **Painkiller**:

    - You can definitely do it. Take a break and think about something else for a while.

    - Allow your previous successes to inspire you.

    - The success of your competitors may be a source of frustration for you, but there are many sources of inspiration within the successes of others, even in aspects far from your area of interest.

    - Remember that achieving your goal from the first trial is not the definition of success. Rather, it is precisely referred to as *luck*. Normally, success comes after several attempts. The outstanding successes are born from the womb of suffering.

- **Treatment**:

    - The recipe's ingredients of luck are not specific, while success's basic component is hard work.

    - Persistence does not necessarily mean repeating the attempts in every detail.

- While it is highly important to be cautious not to repeat your previous mistakes, it is no less important to foresee the possible new snags and be ready to overcome them.

- You achieve your success through determination, not by counting the number of previous attempts. Don't allow yourself to become apprehensive before your upcoming attempt.

BAD LUCK

- **Symptom:** Feeling that you were born unlucky.

- **Diagnosis**: A rare opportunity slips from your hands.

- **Painkiller**:

  - Remember your past successes. You definitely didn't need luck in all of them.

  - Why do you view it as a missed opportunity? There's no guarantee or certainty that you would have hit the ground running if you had the opportunity. Perhaps there are other rare opportunities around you that will achieve multiple successes for you. You just need to pay attention to them and capture them.

  - It's okay if you feel sorry for yourself awhile. Remember that you will be much better the more you try to forget about it. Draw from any lessons learned to continue your work and life effectively.

  - While it is often better not to ruminate on memories of the unpleasant experience, it can sometimes be a good idea to think about some of the negative effects that you did not see from a missed opportunity. This can help you overcome regret and feel more comfortable.

✐ **Treatment**:

- ✐ Don't give in to the saying that a rare opportunity never knocks on your door twice. Do not focus all your attention on a particular rare opportunity. You will find that there are many rare opportunities as you expand your horizons and search every field. With that in mind, you will realize that rare opportunities are endless.

- ✐ Next time it is important to realize that you do not have to wait for only one opportunity, however valuable it may seem. Watch for any other valuable opportunities, and work them parallel to seize them.

- ✐ Success in life is not achieved by waiting for opportunities to seize. Steadfast success is seriously trying to create your own unique opportunities, not just sitting around waiting for them.

- ✐ It is important to realize that we do not choose our fortunes. We work hard and intelligently and let luck choose us.

SATISFYING EVERYONE

- *⊘* **Symptom:** Wishing you could actually split in half.

- *⊘* **Diagnosis**: Struggling to satisfy two disputing, stubborn persons who are close to you.

- *⊘* **Painkiller**:

  - *⊘* No matter how complicated and annoying it seems, remember that someone who is worthy of being close to you should make it easier for you to make a decision in one way or another. He or she should not just sit waiting for your decision as if putting you in a harsh test.

  - *⊘* Get moral and emotional support from someone who does not pressure you during the decision-making and shows understanding. In parallel, do not rush to take actions that might lead to losing totally the relationship with the convulsive person, even if that person seems to warn you against taking a position not in his or her best interest.

  - *⊘* With regard to preserving the relationship and the satisfaction of both parties, remember that the most important thing is to preserve the relationship in the long term. It is good to notice that the transient distress of any party as a result of your decision will have little impact in the long run.

  - *⊘* Beyond the topic of dispute, you will definitely find a way to satisfy the angry party as a result of your decision. Focus carefully on what suits that party and suits you within the reasons for appeasement. Do not rush to make a decision directly; perhaps it is better to allow some time to absorb the anger of the other party so that your appeasement does not seem like a cheap bribe.

✐ **Treatment:**

✐ It is wise to approach the problem calmly and without further provoking either party. But it is important to focus on the problem itself and not sacrifice any aspect of the radical solution to obtain the satisfaction of one of the parties.

✐ You should note that people's satisfaction is not only an unrealizable goal but a purpose that must not be realized in the first place. When you try to please all parties in any case, you will lose a lot of your peace of mind and even some of your principles.

✐ Show intimacy and care about the relationship for both parties. You should not show any party your fear of his or her anger if you make a decision that might satisfy the other party. In order to be successful in this, you must not be afraid of the consequences of any thoughtful decision that you make.

✐ Do not hesitate to take a position that may anger both parties as long as you have considered all the alternatives and did not find a better decision than that position as a fair choice. The situation that angered both parties is not necessarily the worst decision.

✐ Often the failure to make any decision is nothing but an escape from the problem. In doing so, the two parties may get angry, and you end up with worse results than the options you were afraid of.

✐ The more you clear your mind of concerns about pleasing both parties, the faster the optimal solution will emerge.

BETRAYAL

- 🔶 **Symptom**: Complete loss of trust in others.

- 🔶 **Diagnosis**: Betrayal of the first degree.

- 🔶 **Painkiller**:

  - 🔶 It is important to be careful before trusting others. But do not blame yourself too much as there is no guarantee regarding treacherous surprises from others.

  - 🔶 It may take a long time to recover from the experience. To help yourself recover faster, try to get preoccupied with topics completely distant from the incident of betrayal.

  - 🔶 Feel content for stopping further damages by discovering the betrayal and ending the relationship at that limit.

  - 🔶 Be grateful for your relationships that are still maintaining loyalty. But beware of overestimating the value of these relationships.

- 🔶 **Treatment**:

  - 🔶 Avoid the temptation to judge others in light of your tough betrayal experience.

- If this is a repeated betrayal from the same person, the relationship is unlikely to recover.

- If the betrayal case is experienced for the first time from someone, the utmost caution must be exercised with this person in the event of thinking about returning to the relationship.

- It is good in all cases to open wisely fresh parallel and alternative relationships with other people.

- It takes a careful balancing act between more discipline in providing confidence in future relationships and not being overly cautious about others.

FAILURE TO PASS A JOB INTERVIEW

- *Ø* **Symptom**: Either lack of self-confidence in career or likely some level of paranoia.

- *Ø* **Diagnosis**: Losing a critically needed recruitment opportunity subsequent to a remarkable performance on a job interview, likely after a series of similar cases of less severity.

- *Ø* **Painkiller**:

  - *Ø* Remind yourself that others' decisions are their own opinions and not absolute judgments on your abilities.

  - *Ø* Remember how you could overcome all previous similar incidents.

  - *Ø* Be more grateful in your current job, whatever it is.

  - *Ø* Don't hesitate to reward yourself in a childish way, such as enjoying your favorite dessert.

- *Ø* **Treatment**:

  - *Ø* Remember that life is greater and more complex than just being affected by missing one or even a number of chances.

- Try to review your performance carefully and get some lessons to learn, even if they are about how to deal with others' mistakes.

- Allow yourself some time before making a serious decision on your future career.

- Remember that you are always free to change your career at any time.

LOSS OF YOUR JOB

 Symptom: Feeling as though you won't be able to secure your next meal.

 Diagnosis: Getting fired from your job, regardless of the polite terms other people use in front of you to describe the incident.

 Painkiller:

- Remember that you were surviving before getting that job.

- Take it as an opportunity to go for a better job.

- Implement on the spot a plan to squeeze your spending.

- Utilize your past relationships account to find a new job carefully and wisely.

- Introduce yourself to encourage those expected to help you get a better job as an added value for those who will hire you.

 Treatment:

- Do not rush to accept the fastest-arriving job opportunity without a careful evaluation.

- Focus on seizing this forced chance of getting a better job.

- If you are forced to accept a less-satisfying job opportunity, make sure it is temporary with a clearly specified and strict time frame.

- It is not necessarily the last tough experience. Clearly study the lessons learned and be better prepared for possible sudden job-loss experiences in the future.

RETIREMENT

- **Symptom:** Feeling as if it is the end of the world.

- **Diagnosis**: The period around retirement date.

- **Painkiller**:

  - Avoid feeling as if what happened was a surprise.

  - Start implementing your plans for this day, however difficult it currently may seem.

  - Get inspired by the positive examples shown by those who have gone through the experience before you.

  - Don't be surprised when you find yourself accomplishing a lot of your retirement work and plans in weeks or even a few days.

- **Treatment**:

  - Saving is important, but it is always better to spend from good investment returns rather than from excellent savings.

- Knowing what to keep yourself busy with after retirement is just as important as planning your budget and expenses after retirement.

- Let go the frustration of being ignored by those who used to seek your attention and request your support when you were in the seat of authority.

- Be flexible so that you keep your agenda busy by creating appropriate new tasks as needed.

- Pay special attention to social commitments, and be keen to fulfill them.

- Remember that it may be the toughest challenge you face against flexibility, and do your best to overcome that challenge.

A ROMANTIC RELATIONSHIP ENDS

Symptom: Viewing friendship as the most trivial relationship and feeling that life is of no use.

Diagnosis: Your lover asked to continue the relationship as friends.

Painkiller:

- Denial is the painkiller with the most harmful side effects; stop it at the earliest.

- Beware of immediate reactions urging you to go into a compensatory relationship.

- Avoid revealing your weakness, and beware dragging other people's sympathy.

- Make sure to communicate with close people you trust. Expand the circle of your communication with trustworthy people who have no connection with the problem to get a deep refreshment.

Treatment:

- Time, time, and time.

- When you feel balanced to go into a fresh experience, your new relationship will be better if you are neither looking for a replica of the old one nor the absolute opposite.

🖊 Do not overthink. In love relationships, separation is not always due to a mistake by either party. The issue is often incompatibility in moods or visions.

🖊 You will make the biggest mistake when you give up and deliberately choose not to enter any new relationship in anticipation of a potential failure.

THE DEMISE OF A CLOSE PERSON

- **Symptom:** Repeating the question: Why am I still alive?

- **Diagnosis:** The demise of a dear person.

- **Painkiller**:

  - Breakdown is neither good for you nor returns the loss.

  - Remember that passing away is the destiny of every living creature at the same level, not only for a person close to you.

  - Keep doing what your deceased loved one liked you doing.

  - Realize and be grateful for the grace of your loved ones still living.

- **Treatment:**

  - It is hard to digest, but it is good to remember that extinction is life's nature, and we have no control over it.

- You will not forget, and you should never forget. Just make sure to remember in the best way for you and others around.

- Work carefully and intelligently to retrieve memories that give you strength and comfort.

- From time to time, it is okay to feel as if the loss happened recently. Allow your feelings to flow spontaneously and without prolongation or exaggeration.

INJUSTICE

○ **Symptom:** You keep repeating the question: Is there not a rational man?

○ **Diagnosis**: The guilty is acquitted, and the charges are proved against you without any firm evidence.

○ **Painkiller:**

   ○ Be closer to loyal friends. They will inspire you to stand firm and face people with courage.

   ○ Remember that absolute justice is impossible.

   ○ Stay calm, and don't overshow your determination to continue fighting.

   ○ Your loss does not mean that everyone is against you. People often tend to be passive when observing problems, but they mostly know which side is right.

○ **Treatment:**

   ○ Do not rely fundamentally on people's opinions and reactions as a mainstay of your principles and positions.

- In general, avoid teasing and peeving as a main tactic in your confrontations with your opponents. That helps you to ignore the effect of the superficial passive emotional reactions from others when you lose a battle.

- Work smartly on your case, not just enthusiastically.

- Continue to stand up for yourself and prove you're right. Not the unfair judgment but surrender is the defeat.

- It is difficult for anyone to get out of any battle completely losing. Try to extract some of what you gained from the battle, and think of taking advantage of that to win the next battles.

AN INTRIGUE

Symptom: Feeling as if you were deluded your whole lifetime.

Diagnosis: A big misunderstanding with a lifetime friend due to an intrigue by a jealous new friend.

Painkiller:

- Cross-check it. You may discover that you have wrongly evaluated what or overreacted to what is communicated to you.

- Even if you still believe him or her guilty, remember the good qualities of your lifetime friend and his or her loyal attitudes toward you.

- Avoid revealing your overreactions to the new friend.

- Never give in to the pleasure of submissiveness to the feeling of the victim who has been betrayed. This is a passive reaction and will not benefit anything or anyone. Whatever the details of circumstances, take the initiative to move practically in any direction in a positive way.

Treatment:

- Do not worry, and do not hurry. If the basis of the relationship is solid, it will heal in a satisfactory way, even if slowly.

- It is good to handle the case mainly with careful, wise consideration of people and evaluation of relationships through different circumstances in life, rather than being obsessed with identifying and judging good people and bad people, especially when it comes to an old relationship.

- If things are not sorted out spontaneously after a while, allow for open discussions with your lifetime friend, regardless of how far you believe he or she is responsible for the misunderstanding.

- If all steps to restore the relationship do not work, then this is not the end of the world. It is also important to pay attention to the necessity of preserving the history of pure old bonds and good memories. If it turns out that the relationship cannot continue as it was, this does not mean it should be completely destroyed.

AHEAD OF YOUR TIME

- **Symptom:** Believing that you are living in the wrong time or wrong place.

- **Diagnosis**: Nobody understands or responds to you as you expect.

- **Painkiller**:

  - Stay confident. Even if you are really in the wrong time or wrong place, it doesn't mean that you are the wrong person.

  - Don't worry. You don't necessarily need to change any of your opinions; it's just how you present those opinions to others.

  - If you are confident in your ideas, but it is difficult for you to change the way you deliver these ideas, you can still cope with all that in your life. You can communicate effectively with people through other parallel channels and approaches in various walks of life. What is between human beings in life is certainly not a single issue.

  - Think of communicating your thoughts and opinions to others as if providing a service to them. It will become easier, and you may find it enjoyable.

🗪 **Treatment:**

- 🗪 The matter has nothing necessarily to do with your capabilities or the capabilities of others, not even the intentions of any of the parties. You must take steps to bring your views closer to others, even if this calls for some sensible concessions.

- 🗪 You cannot change your time, but you can certainly change the place. This does not necessarily require that you migrate; just try to address a different class of people or switch to another field of work.

- 🗪 It will not hurt or diminish your value if you try to respond to what others expect of you as long as that does not clearly clash with any of your principles.

- 🗪 If you are firmly convinced that your thoughts are ahead of their time and you cannot abandon them, then work with patience, wisdom, and skill to consolidate those thoughts so that they are truly influential for a later era. Avoid wasting your energy in central fights or side quarrels.

CASCADE OF PROBLEMS

🔍 **Symptom:** Feeling that the whole world is hostile to you.

🔍 **Diagnosis**: Coincidentally, you have encountered several consecutive problems with scattered groups of people, among them some close to you.

🔍 **Painkiller**:

   🔍 Raise your head and look around. You will see many supporters and devotees regardless of the number of people you believe hate you and the problems you have fallen into.

   🔍 The cascade of problems exposes those with fragile friendships and reveals the opportunists. Use this as one of the benefits of the harsh experience but without overreacting to those who give up supporting you.

   🔍 Your great wisdom in dealing with worsening problems makes some opponents change their positions by giving up the attack on you. It undoubtedly makes almost everyone respect you.

   🔍 The more patient and wise you are during the cascade of problems, the more rewards you will win. There is an existential law that is rarely mistaken: Cruel problems are followed by a great breakthrough.

Treatment:

- Do not be tempted by a conspiracy theory. Conspiracies do exist, but overthinking them is a barrier to overcoming problems and continuing properly with life.

- The conspirators deserve more attention from you. Deal with them with patience and discernment; it will not help you to hate them and be hostile to them.

- It is very important to pay attention to the significance of not connecting cascading problems to each other. Try to avoid holding someone involved in one problem responsible for another problem just because you suspect the matter. That behavior will multiply the loss in the long run.

- Sometimes all you need is to pause. The insistence on tackling impulsively cascading problems leads mostly to exacerbating them.

DEFEAT

- **Symptom:** A deep feeling of refraction.

- **Diagnosis**: Losing in a significant intellectual or physical spar.

- **Painkiller**:

  - The more you regain the bitterness of defeat and the more you remember the reactions of those you know, the more difficult the healing and recovery will be. Remember the incident only for the sake of drawing lessons from it. Self-flagellation will not do you any good.

  - Defeat may be bitter, but it must not be destructive. You have the right to be upset, but pay attention; your collapse is not justified.

  - Remember that you neither lost a war nor even a battle; it is just a spar. Everyone will forget your loss and remember your cohesion and subsequent victories.

  - Transient losses are exasperating when you make them bigger than their actual size. Many people will intentionally and unintentionally motivate you in that direction. All you need is to put the spar in its rightful place within your broad life framework. If you succeed in that, the side effects of the loss, no matter how bitter they are, will disappear automatically.

✑ **Treatment:**

- ✑ It is important to charge yourself with the utmost psychological energy to enhance confidence in achieving victory before and during the preparation for the spar. But it is generally wise to realize that every encounter in life has win and loss potentials.

- ✑ It is wise not to immerse yourself in every spar by responding to all sent signals, whether being provoked by others or as a result of self-enthusiasm. Carefully study the consequences and benefits of the spar for you, and make the decision accordingly.

- ✑ When defeated in a spar, do not fear the next confrontation, and do not rush it to happen. Just leave it for the time as you may not need to confront again in a direct way to restore your dignity and feel rehabilitated.

- ✑ Focus on planning your coming achievement smartly. Work with determination and confidence to achieve long-lasting success, not just a fast-acting victory.

ABANDON PRINCIPLES

🔘 **Symptom:** A sharp feeling of pangs of conscience.

🔘 **Diagnosis**: Abandon some principles in an awkward situation.

🔘 **Painkiller**:

   🔘 A prick of conscience means that you tried following principles before stepping in. Whatever it is, continuing to feel guilty for so long will not change anything already perpetrated. Do not hesitate to take any immediate appropriate action to correct the situation as far as possible.

   🔘 Avoid begging for excuses from those around you to feel comfortable. Seek advice from people you trust about what can be done to remedy the situation. Draw from lessons learned to help you with upcoming challenges.

   🔘 Turn all your regret for bypassing principles into an insistence on sticking to them in the coming times.

   🔘 Perfection is impossible. Make this an incentive for you to approach challenging principles with confidence, skill, and calm. Beware of using this common saying as an excuse for slackness, as then you will fall into aggravating problems rather than easing principles' challenges as some peoples might expect.

⬮ **Treatment:**

- ⬮ Always try to clearly define your principles. Don't allow gray areas as much as possible, but always be willing to show flexibility.

- ⬮ Don't flaunt your principles. Principles are an integrated way of life, not just something to show off occasionally. Embrace what you believe in with calmness, tranquility, and assurance, and you will be able to abide by it with the least number of arguments and controversies possible.

- ⬮ It is always best to be prepared in advance to the test of principles in any encounter. Visualize the expected principles' challenges every time and the ethical approach scenario from your side so that you do not get confused and become hostage to sudden perplexities that force you to make ill-considered compromises.

- ⬮ Principles are an integral approach in life, but they are not a single package. No one is perfect in terms of his or her commitment to all principles. Celebrate and cherish your strengths, and do not be shy to acknowledge your weaknesses to address them. Always remember that the tests the principles impose on you are different and renewed every time, even if the general framework seems to be one.

19

ROUTINE

 Symptom: You want it so badly, yet you fear it at the same level.

 Diagnosis: You are hesitant to take on a new challenge that will add a lot to your life, fearing its great impact on your usual daily routine.

 Painkiller:

 There is no need to hesitate. Every work at its beginning seems confusing and difficult, and then becomes easier the more you get used to it. You will rearrange your life to include a new routine and will become familiar with as well.

 Remember that it is not a one-way road. You can return at any moment, but it is wise not to hasten making a decision to return at the first difficulty you encounter. Give yourself some time, and it will automatically become clear to you which decision is best.

 Even if you were not feeling bored, it is wise to renew and refresh your routine. See the new challenge as an opportunity to inject new life into your everyday details.

 Remember that your current routine will somehow end. It is better if you take the initiative to change it because even if you do not like the experience completely, you will at least get rid of the phobia of stillness and become used to some change.

- Not an exaggeration, but you may actually feel satisfied and happy with the new routine to the extent that you bemoan your delay in taking the change step.

- **Treatment:**

  - It is important not to go overboard in any habit or routine. Enjoy your sweet habits and routines but not to the point of becoming addicted to them in any way.

  - It is good to have your backup plan for any habit or routine ready so that you are not surprised by the emptiness when you can no longer practice a habit or routine you have stuck to for a long time.

  - It is always better to create your own habits and routines. Surrendering to the status quo—no matter how pleasant—makes your habits and routines in the possession of others, given the developments in life that require everyone to deal with changes. Others are changing, and their actions will impact you if you are not, in turn, taking some initiatives.

  - Do not be ashamed of your seemingly embarrassing habits and routines as long as you have done your best toward treating them, and as long as they do not negatively affect others and do not clearly hinder your life. Just be aware that you do not need to show your privacy to others to the point of provoking them to comment on what does not concern them, which may lead to distress and annoy you.

20

SELF-ESTEEM EXAGGERATION

🔖 **Symptom:** Feeling that you deserve more respect and appreciation than you are getting.

🔖 **Diagnosis**: You expect some people to appreciate your stature, even though they know nothing about it.

🔖 **Painkiller**:

- 💊 If you do not notice the attention you expect in a situation, this does not necessarily mean that others ignore you. Recognition and appreciation cannot consistently appear to the same degree from all people all the time.

- 💊 If someone who meets you for the first time ignores you, it is because he does not know your stature. And if someone who knows you deliberately ignores you, then that individual does not deserve to care for him or her. A person worthy of your feelings and emotions will appreciate you anyway.

- 💊 Responding reciprocatively to someone who ignored you may make you feel the pleasure of revenge. That's okay, but don't overly show indifference to the person who ignored you in front of others.

- 💊 Whenever you encounter a situation in which you are being ignored, use it as a coercive opportunity to practice humility. Whatever your nature, you need such exercise, and it will be very helpful when you take it seriously.

◯ **Treatment**:

    ◯ Appreciation and recognition from others are undoubtedly important, but your stature is not validated by one or a few situations. Maintain your steadfastness when exposed to a situation that is not satisfactory to your pride so that the situation passes fleetingly. Otherwise your complexity of one fleeting situation may have obvious negative effects on your stature in the long run.

    ◯ Completely avoid showing off and, preemptively, talking about your social standing in order to gain the respect of others. Such behavior will not solve any expected problems about others ignoring or belittling you. On the contrary, it will exacerbate your feelings of frustration and annoyance in the event that you are unintentionally or intentionally ignored or belittled by others in any situation.

    ◯ Be careful not to let your excessive attention for recognition lead you to belittle or ignore others.

    ◯ If you do not provide others with the material or moral support they need, your stature, no matter how high it is, will not concern them.

    ◯ Ways of recognition vary according to different times and societies. Pay attention to your actions to suit the appreciation you expect from the society that includes you at the time that surrounds you.

21

AGING

🔘 **Symptom:** You seem astonished and frustrated, as if you didn't know this was going to happen.

🔘 **Diagnosis**: Feeling the effects of aging are imminent, or that some signs of aging are already showing.

🔘 **Painkiller**:

🔘 There is automatic and ongoing emotional support you can receive by monitoring those close to you who are aging well.

🔘 Get inspiration from the stories of the best people of all time who aged well, not only with regard to their ages' record numbers but also regarding their lifestyles and positive, optimistic behaviors throughout their lives.

🔘 Focus on remembering and evoking the benefits of aging, such as increased respect from others, deep experience in the various aspects of life, and dealing with things with peace and wisdom.

🔘 Try always to stay calm and relaxed; time is not going backward anyway. It is never a problem to relive and enjoy the memories of a beautiful past, but there is no need for the younger people to be repulsed by repeating to them that they missed living during that beautiful time. This behavior may complicate matters as the younger people do not share your opinion. Rather, they are more likely to see the opposite of what you see.

- You can slow down the speed of life while it progresses only by prolonging your enjoyment of the good and beautiful moments in which you live. Extract the maximum contentment out of these moments, and take that with you as an inspiring memory.

- **Treatment:**

  - The most effective approach for dealing with the obsession of aging is seriously training yourself in advance to enjoy each stage of life by adopting the means and lifestyle that suit your age at each phase.

  - It is a good idea to adapt your habits and lifestyle to suit your age group. Beware not to take denial as an involuntary means of cling on to youth. Self-moral stimulation is beneficial psychologically and physically, but denial will in no way help fool your body.

  - Your advanced age and experience do not mean that you no longer need the advice or expertise of others. Take the initiative to do so, and do not hesitate to learn and gain inspiration from those who are younger and lower in stature than you are. Contrary to what you might think, you will find they have a lot from which you can learn and benefit.

  - Take care of yourself, and always be optimistic. Take continuous proactive and preventive steps to preserve the manifestations of your youth in form and substance. Do not hesitate to take into account the preparation of a clear and practical ideation of how you will behave toward unpleasant scenarios when they happen.

WHIRLPOOL

🗿 **Symptom:** Feeling that you are in a whirlpool you will not be able to get out of.

🗿 **Diagnosis**: Repetition of the same life's problems after you think you passed them.

🗿 **Painkiller**:

  🗿 It will likely be strange and upsetting to sit for high school exams after graduating from college and practicing a working life for years. But if you find yourself forced to, it is best to do it confidently and enthusiastically. Resenting and complaining will not help you pass the test.

  🗿 Problems and difficulties do not repeat themselves in every detail. Seize the opportunity and savor the thrill of a special challenge by discovering the different details each time and trying to find innovative solutions that suit them.

  🗿 Recurring problems definitely make you feel monotonous and malaise, but see your accumulated experience in similar challenges as a great point of strength in dealing with these problems with greater confidence and optimism about your success.

  🗿 Life's difficulties are not in the form of tests that you succeed in one of them and overcome to enter the next. Consider the overlap of problems, their repetition, and their rotation as opportunities for humility. And remember that no one in life is above any test, regardless of his or her stature.

ℰ **Treatment:**

    ℰ It doesn't look like an endless loop, but life is actually an endless loop that you have to get adapted to.

    ℰ Your adaptation to the spiral of life is best achieved through your deep belief that this is the nature of existence. This does not mean that you stand submissively in front of any problem. But the issues that recur and the vicious circles of life are not problems as much as realistic and uninterrupted challenges that require a lot of patience, wisdom, and longanimity to deal with them.

    ℰ Although problems are not repeated with the same details, drawing inspiration from previous solutions to a similar problem is not without benefit. Make sure you evoke old solutions with an open sprit eager to resolve the problem, not only to clear your guilt and relax your conscience by just trying.

    ℰ Expand the scope of your activities on all levels. Relying on a routine does not spare you problems so much as it may help them to recur. Renewable activities refresh your life. Just make sure that you choose them carefully from among what suits you.

Printed in the United States
by Baker & Taylor Publisher Services